SPEEDWAY BIKES

MOTORCYCLE MANIA

David and Patricia Armentrout

Rourke
Publishing LLC
Vero Beach, Florida 32964

www.rourkepublishing.com

PHOTO CREDITS: All images ©Mike Patrick

Title page: *Speedway racers line up at the start.*

Editor: Frank Sloan

Cover and page design by Nicola Stratford

Library of Congress Cataloging-in-Publication Data

Armentrout, David, 1962-
  Speedway bikes / David and Patricia Armentrout.
      p. cm. -- (Motorcycle mania)
  Includes bibliographical references and index.
  ISBN 1-59515-455-8 (hardcover)
  1. Superbikes--Juvenile literature. I. Armentrout, Patricia, 1960- II.
Title. III. Series.
  TL440.15.A76 2006
  629.227'5--dc22
                              2005010710

Printed in the USA

CG/CG

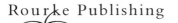

Rourke Publishing
1-800-394-7055
www.rourkepublishing.com
sales@rourkepublishing.com
Post Office Box 3328, Vero Beach, FL 32964

TABLE OF CONTENTS

SPEEDWAY-THE EXTREME WAY

Speedway is a basic form of dirt track racing. That's not to say speedway is easy. Speedway racing is physically challenging, and it can be dangerous. Riders must be in top form to compete in this extreme motor sport.

Riders scramble for the lead position as they enter the first turn.

Speedway is a global sport that is most popular in Europe. Speedway races, called **heats**, take place both indoors and out. Riders race on oval tracks ranging from 250 to 425 meters in length. The track surface is usually loosely packed **shale**, but it can be dirt, grass, or even ice.

The FIM (Federation Internationale de Motorcyclisme), based in Geneva, Switzerland, is the worldwide governing body for motorcycle sport and touring activity.

It takes great skill to race in wet, muddy conditions.

THE BIKES

Speedway motorcycles are sturdy, but light, weighing about 185 pounds (84 kilograms). They run on a highly explosive fuel called **methanol**.

The **acceleration** of a speedway bike is often compared to that of a Formula One racing car. Top riders go from zero to 60 in under 3 seconds and reach speeds greater than 80 miles (129 kilometers) an hour on the straightaways.

A rider pulls a wheelie as he rockets out of the gate.

Speedway bikes have no gears, brakes, or rear suspension. They do have a footrest mounted low on the right side of the bike, but not on the left. This is because riders always go **counterclockwise** and lean into the curves. Riders slide the rear tire sideways around the turns (called a power slide) and control their speed by dragging their left foot along the ground.

Speedway riders have a steel plate on the bottom of their left boot to keep it from wearing away.

A perfect power slide requires complete control.

THE ENGINE

The heaviest part of a speedway bike is the engine. Speedway bikes use powerful 500 cc, or **cubic centimeter**, single-**cylinder** four-stroke engines. This means the piston in the cylinder moves four times to produce power.

How a four-stroke engine works:
1. On the first downstroke of the piston, gas and air are sucked into the engine.
2. The piston rises and compresses the fuel on the second stroke.
3. The spark plug explodes the fuel and forces the piston down on the third stroke.
4. On the fourth stroke, the piston moves up and forces out exhaust gases.

The engine's position on the frame gives the bike a low center of gravity.

THE HEATS

A speedway meet will run approximately 20 heats. A typical heat pits four riders against each other—two riders from two different teams. They race four laps around the track, hoping to reach the black-and-white checkered flag before the opposition.

Speedway is typically a team sport, but some organizations hold individual competitions.

A large crowd watches as racers leave the gate.

Fans love the drama and excitement. They sit on the edge of their seats waiting for wipeouts as riders power slide around the turns. It's over in less than a minute, and, in the end, the team with the most points wins.

Point System
Finish first—3 points
Finish second—2 points
Finish third—1 point
Finish fourth—0 points

Speedway racers don't mind taking time to greet fans.

GRIPPING THE ICE

If you think speedway events sound exciting, you should experience ice speedway. A frozen oval track makes all the difference. Ice bikes are like regular speedway bikes, with the exception of two fierce-looking tires. Because rubber tires slide on the frozen track, ice racers have about 300 1-inch-(2.5-centimeters-) long spikes screwed into their tires to grip the ice.

For safety reasons, guards cover both tires to prevent the spikes from jabbing other riders.

Riders collide during the last heat of the meet.

Ice heats are similar to regular speedway races. One difference is that riders don't power slide the rear tire around corners. Instead, they lean into the bends, sometimes scraping the ice with the left handlebar.

Both speedway and ice speedway are motor sports that require specialized bikes and equipment. Racing is not for everyone, but the thrill and excitement of a speedway event can be!

Spiked tires give bikes traction on slippery ice.

A BIT OF SPEEDWAY HISTORY

Did you know that Speedway got its start "down under?" That's right, Australians turned American dirt track racing of the early 1900s into a whole new sport. The Aussies refined dirt track racing and invented the art of power sliding around 1925.

By 1928, organized Speedway meetings were taking place in England. Leagues began to sprout up all over, and by 1950 Speedway had became one of Britain's largest spectator sports. Wildly popular today, Spcedway enthusiasts around the world compete for the ultimate title in Speedway World Championship events.

A rider hits the dirt after his bike sheds a chain.

GLOSSARY

acceleration (ak SEL uh RAY shun) — speeding up, going faster and faster

counterclockwise (KOUN tur KLOK wize) — the direction opposite to which the hands of a clock rotate

cubic centimeter (KYOO bik SENT uh mee tur) — a measurement of volume in the metric system that tells us how much space is inside an engine

cylinder (SIL un dur) — a chamber in an engine shaped like a tube that holds the piston as it moves up and down

heats (HEETZ) — speedway races on oval tracks

methanol (METH uh NOL) — a highly explosive fuel

shale (SHAYL) — rock formed from hardened clay or mud that splits easily into layers

INDEX

FURTHER READING

Hill, Lee Sullivan. *Motorcycles*. Lerner Publications, 2004.
Morris, Mark. *Motorbikes: Mean Machine*. Raintree, 2004.

WEBSITES TO VISIT

Canada and USA Speedway Motorcycle Racing
   www.speedwaybikes.com/
American Motorcyclist Association
   ama-cycle.org
FIM
   www.fim.ch/

ABOUT THE AUTHORS

David and Patricia Armentrout specialize in writing nonfiction books for young readers. They have had several books published for primary school reading. The Armentrouts live in Cincinnati, Ohio, with their two children.